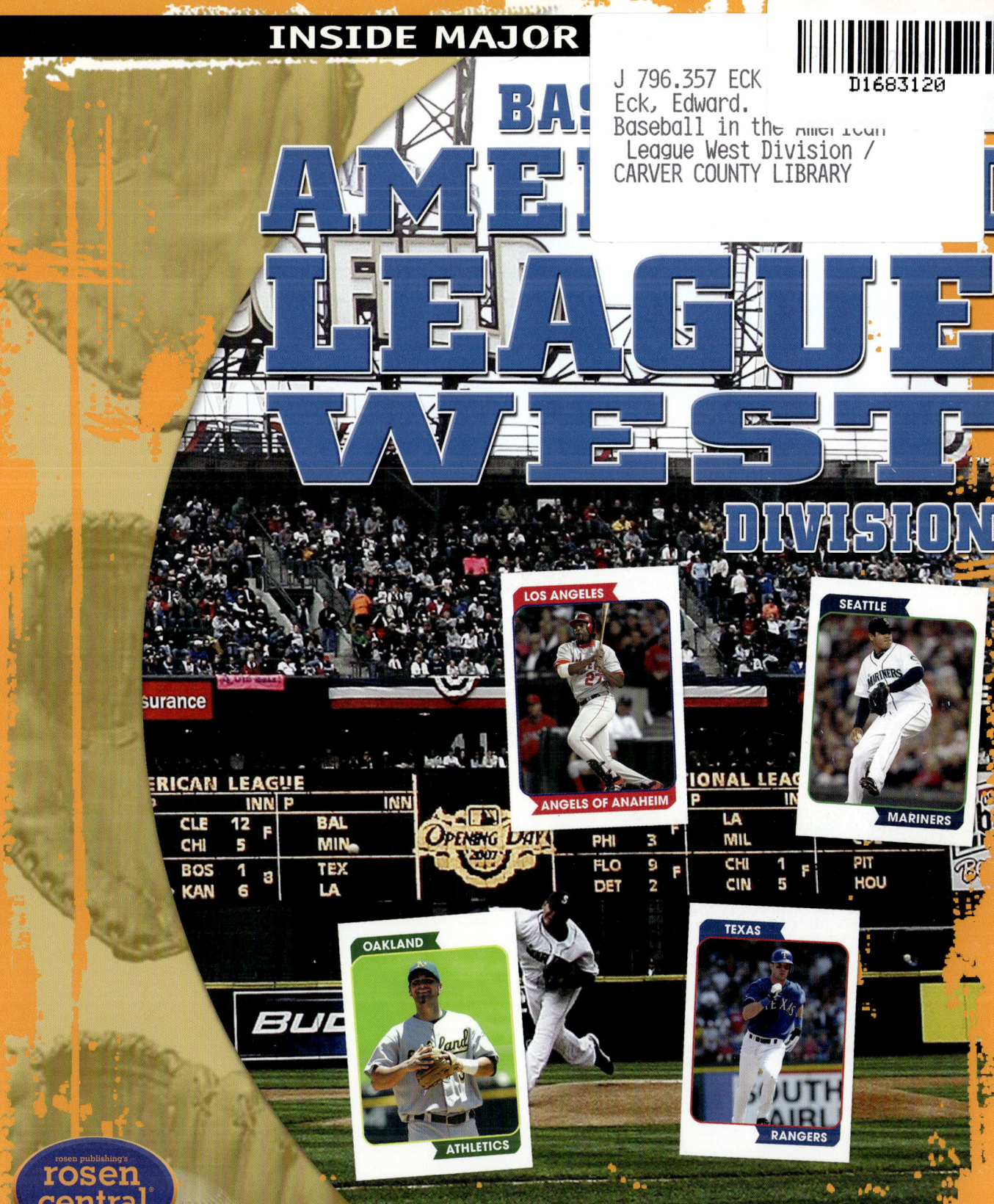

Published in 2009 by The Rosen Publishing Group, Inc.
29 East 21st Street, New York, NY 10010

Copyright © 2009 by The Rosen Publishing Group, Inc.

First Edition

All rights reserved. No part of this book may be reproduced in any form without permission in writing from the publisher, except by a reviewer.

**Library of Congress Cataloging-in-Publication Data**

Eck, Edward.
Baseball in the American League West Division / Edward Eck.—1st ed.
   p. cm.—(Inside major league baseball)
Includes bibliographical references and index.
ISBN-13: 978-1-4358-5041-5 (library binding)
ISBN-13: 978-1-4358-5415-4 (pbk)
ISBN-13: 978-1-4358-5421-5 (6 pack)
1. American League of Professional Baseball Clubs—Juvenile literature. 2. Baseball teams—West (U.S.)—Juvenile literature. I. Title.
GV875.A15E35 2009
796.357'640973—dc22

                                                                                    2008025408

*Manufactured in the United States of America*

**On the cover:** Baseball cards, top to bottom: Vladimir Guerrero of the Anaheim Angels of Los Angeles; Eric Chavez of the Oakland A's; Félix Hernández of the Seattle Mariners; Michael Young of the Texas Rangers. Foreground: Seattle Mariners' Ichiro Suzuki connects with a pitch. Background: Seattle Mariners' Safeco Field.

# CONTENTS

**INTRODUCTION** — 4

**CHAPTER ONE**
**History of the AL West Division** — 7

**CHAPTER TWO**
**The Players** — 14

**CHAPTER THREE**
**Memorable Games** — 26

**CHAPTER FOUR**
**Ballparks and Traditions** — 30

**GLOSSARY** — 40

**FOR MORE INFORMATION** — 41

**FOR FURTHER READING** — 43

**BIBLIOGRAPHY** — 44

**INDEX** — 47

# INTRODUCTION

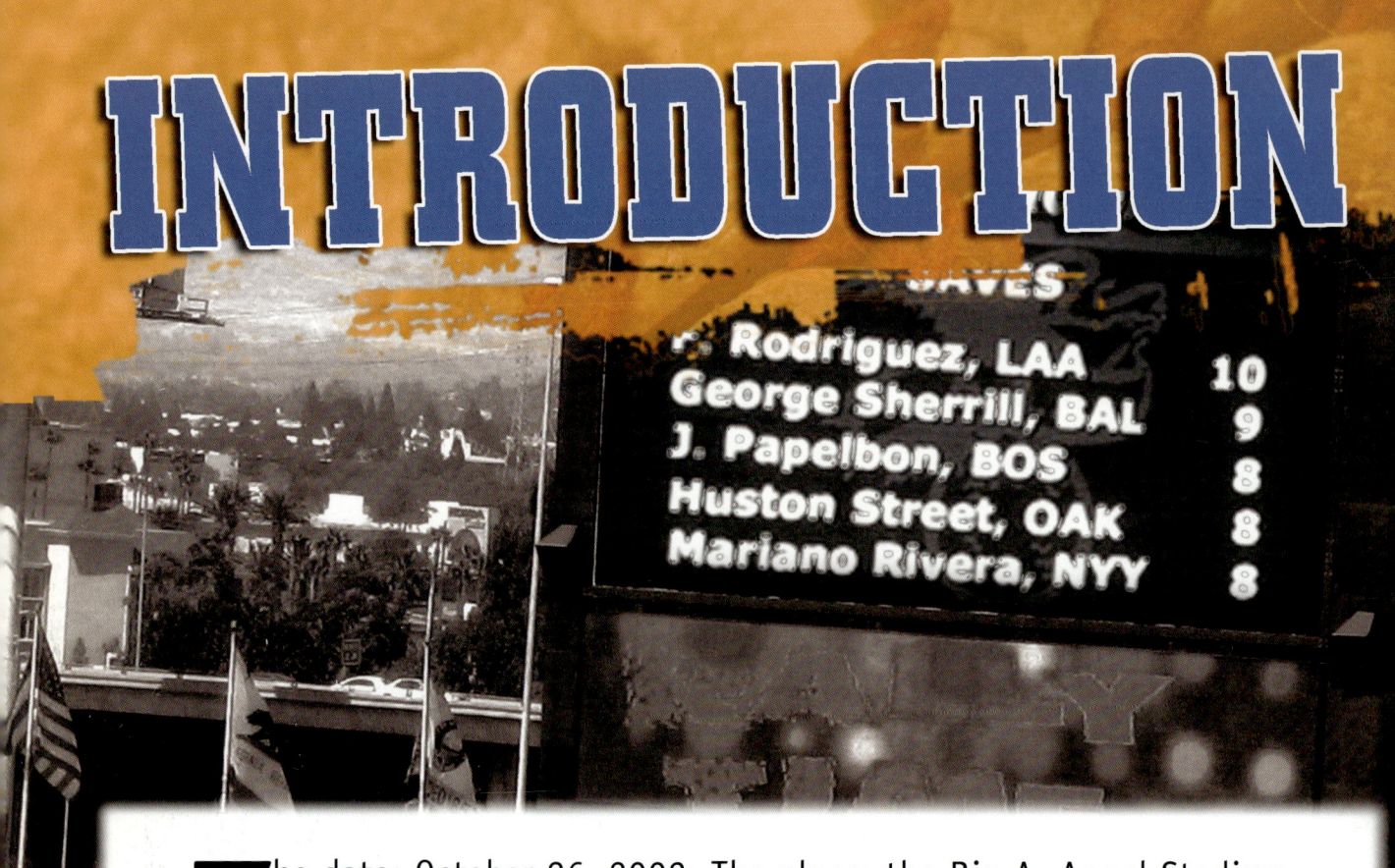

The date: October 26, 2002. The place: the Big A, Angel Stadium of Anaheim, in California. The scene: the home team Anaheim Angels are trailing the San Francisco Giants three games to two in the World Series. If the Giants win the game, they will be crowned champs.

In the seventh inning, with San Francisco ahead 5–0, ballpark officials give the word to start preparing the Giants' clubhouse for the champagne-soaked celebration that seems all but certain. But there is one thing the Giants aren't counting on: the Rally Monkey.

All season long, when the Angels trailed late in a game, the huge scoreboard above the right-field bleachers would flash an image of a real capuchin monkey. It held a sign that said either "Believe in the Power of the Rally Monkey" or "Rally Time!!!" And all season long it worked to get the crowd fired up and involved in the game. When the monkey appears on the scoreboard in the seventh inning of game 6, the sellout crowd of 44,506 goes nuts.

# RALLY TIME !!!

The Rally Monkey goes right to work. Angels third baseman, Troy Glaus, and first baseman, Brad Fulmer, lead off the inning with singles. Then, Scott Spiezio steps to the plate. Giants pitcher Felix Rodriguez quickly gets two strikes on the Angels' second baseman. Behind on the count, Spiezio really digs his heels in, fouling off several potential third strikes. When Rodriguez serves up a pitch on the inside part of the plate, Spiezio swings hard and smacks a high fly ball that sails over the right fielder's head and lands . . . in the stands. A three-run homer! The Angels creep within two runs.

In the eighth inning, the Rally Monkey makes another inspirational appearance. Before long, Glaus is up again, doubling in two runs and giving the

Background: The Rally Monkey gets the crowd pumped up at Angel Stadium of Anaheim. Above: Angels' pitcher Francisco Rodriguez was one of the Angels' stars in the 2002 World Series.

Angels a lead they will not give up. The Giants' championship celebration has to be put back on ice.

The following night, the Angels win again, this time by a score of 4–1, taking the series four games to three. The victory marks the first time a wild card team from the American League has ever gone all the way to win the World Series. (And it is the first time ever that a monkey plays such a big role in vaulting a team to the top!)

The Angels play in the American League West division. In the first half of the 1970s, the best team in baseball, the Oakland A's, played in the AL West division. Since the mid-1970s, however, the division has produced only a few world champs—the Kansas City Royals in 1985, the Oakland A's in 1989, and the Minnesota Twins in 1987 and 1991. The Royals and Twins no longer play in the American League West. Along with the Chicago White Sox, they moved out of the AL West into the American League Central division when it was created in 1994.

Teams in the American League West now include the Angels, the Oakland A's, the Texas Rangers, and the Seattle Mariners. In the last few decades, these teams have featured some of the greatest players in the game, both pitchers and position players. Read on to learn more about these teams, the history of their division, and the exciting baseball they play in the wild, wild AL West.

# CHAPTER ONE
# HISTORY OF THE AL WEST DIVISION

American League baseball dates back to 1901. However, the West division of the American League is a much more recent creation. Until 1968, the American League was a unified league. This meant that only the team with the best record at the end of the regular season made it to the postseason. That team played against the winner of the National League in the World Series. For more than 60 years, baseball fans were satisfied

*Above, left: Minnesota Twins' All-Star slugger Harmon Killebrew follows through on a swing. From 1969 to 1993, the Twins played in the American League West division.*

with this arrangement. It guaranteed that the World Series would be played by the two best, battle-tested teams in baseball. But as major league baseball expanded and spread to new cities, it became clear that the sport would be better off if more teams had a chance to play in the postseason.

## The American League Gets Split

The major leagues chose to do away with the traditional format following the 1968 season. The American and National leagues both divided their 12 teams into two six-team divisions, East and West. A best-of-five League Championship Series (LCS) was added to the postseason to determine the teams that would meet in the World Series. Dividing the league into divisions meant that more teams could be in contention for the play-offs as the season entered the final weeks of play. Divisions made the game more exciting and brought more fans into the seats.

For the 1969 season, the AL West division was made up of the Oakland A's, Los Angeles Angels, Seattle Pilots, Chicago White Sox, Kansas City Royals, and Minnesota Twins. Over the next several years, the division underwent a couple of changes. For instance, in 1970, the Pilots moved to Milwaukee and became the Brewers. Then, in 1972, the Texas Rangers joined the West division, and the Brewers were bumped into the AL East.

## The Early Years

The Minnesota Twins won the first two AL West division titles, in 1969 and 1970. Their team had one of the best lineups in baseball, with

## Charles O. Finley—The P. T. Barnum of Baseball

Baseball in the early days of the American League West was fun and unpredictable. One of the team executives who stood out in this regard was Athletics owner Charlie Finley. The brash Finley was roundly despised by the A's players. However, he was a dynamic owner and a real baseball innovator.

For instance, after moving his Athletics from Kansas City to Oakland in 1968, Finley decided to bring a little flair to his team. He changed uniform colors to very nontraditional bright gold and green, with white cleats. Players on other teams thought the A's looked like clowns, but many teams now wear bright, eye-catching colors that look better on television.

In addition, Finley was one of the most vocal supporters of the designated hitter. This was an innovation adopted by the American League but not the National League. The designated hitter rule allowed a slugger to replace a typically weak-hitting pitcher in the batting lineup. The designated hitter led to higher scores and, many believe, made the American League more fun to watch.

Finley also built a huge scoreboard that exploded when an A's player hit a homer, and he hired pretty "ball girls" to chase down foul balls. All of this was intended to make the game more exciting and interesting for the fans. Perhaps Finley's best-known gimmick was offering his players bonus money to grow wild mustaches and let their hair grow long. So many players took Finley up on the offer that the team became known as the "Mustache Gang."

Oakland Athletics' relief pitcher Rollie Fingers shows off his trademark handlebar mustache. Fingers was a key member of the A's championship teams in the early 1970s.

hitting machines Tony Oliva and Rod Carew batting in front of Hall of Fame slugger Harmon Killebrew. Following the Twins' run, the AL West was dominated by the powerhouse Oakland A's. They won five consecutive division titles, from 1971 to 1975. In addition, the A's went on to win the World Series in three of those years (1972, 1973, and 1974). Top players from those great A's teams included Reggie Jackson, Rollie Fingers, Jim "Catfish" Hunter, and Vida Blue.

## The AL West Hits Its Stride

Between 1976 and 1980, the Kansas City Royals won the AL West title four times. Unfortunately for them, they were not able to capture a World Series title during this stretch. For the 1977 season, the West division expanded to include the Seattle Mariners. After expansion, the AL West remained unchanged for nearly two decades, with its teams being the Mariners, Oakland A's, California Angels, Chicago White Sox, Kansas City Royals, and Minnesota Twins. From 1977 to 1993, these seven teams played against each other 18 times a year during the regular season, laying the foundations of some heated rivalries that continue to this day.

    In 1985, the Royals, led by star third baseman George Brett, finally won their first world title, beating the St. Louis Cardinals in the World Series. Later in the 1980s, the Oakland A's came to dominate the AL West once again. Their tough pitching staff was led by starter Dave Stewart and Hall of Fame closer Dennis Eckersley. At the plate, the A's featured Mark McGwire and Jose Canseco—the Bash Brothers. McGwire burst on the scene in 1987, smashing 49 home runs to break the rookie record. The following year, Canseco became the first "40-40 man" (at least 40 homers and 40 stolen bases in the same season). The A's won division titles each year from 1988 to 1990. In 1989, the A's went on to a four-game sweep over the cross-bay rival San Francisco Giants in the World Series.

The Minnesota Twins, too, played exciting baseball during this time. They were led by perennial All-Star center fielder Kirby Puckett. The team brought the World Series trophy home to the Humphrey Metrodome twice, in 1987 and again in 1991.

## The Current System

The 1994 season was a watershed year in baseball history. First, the season began with a realignment that created a new division in each league, the Central division. Another play-off round was added, as the three division winners plus one wild card team from each league would now play for the right to advance to the League Championship Series. The wild card team, which could come from any division, was the second-place team with the best win-loss record.

Former American League West teams from Cleveland, Kansas City, and Minnesota were split off to join the Central division. This left the

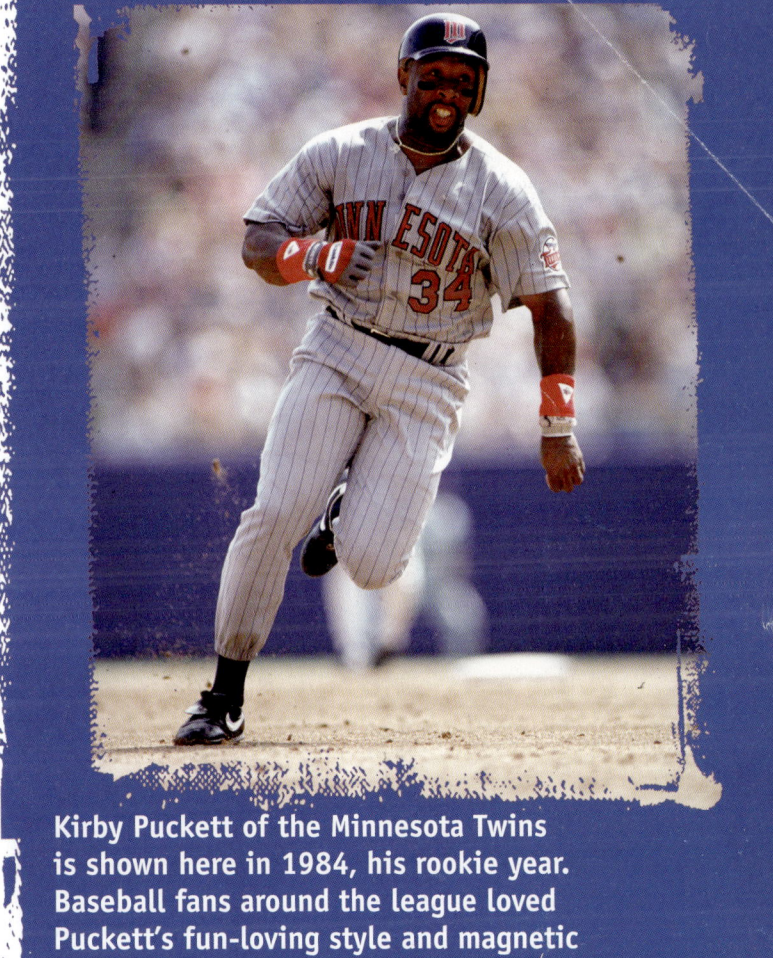

Kirby Puckett of the Minnesota Twins is shown here in 1984, his rookie year. Baseball fans around the league loved Puckett's fun-loving style and magnetic personality.

West with the California Angels, Oakland Athletics, Seattle Mariners, and Texas Rangers.

Unfortunately, the first season with the new system ended up a fiasco. Salary disputes led the Major League Players' Union to go on strike in August 1994, just as the play-off races were heating up. When the dispute could not be settled quickly, the league was forced to cancel the rest of the regular season games, the league play-offs, and the World Series as well. The strike carried on into the beginning of the 1995 season.

## Struggles Out West

Since 1994, teams from the AL West division have not fared too well in the postseason. As of 2007, the division has not produced an American League champion other than the 2002 wild card Angels. However, baseball runs in cycles, so it is probably just a matter of time before the AL West rises once again.

## 2000 and Beyond

Since 2000, the AL West division has been dominated

### American League West Champs
(since realignment in 1994)

1994: Texas Rangers*
1995: Seattle Mariners
1996: Texas Rangers
1997: Seattle Mariners
1998: Texas Rangers
1999: Texas Rangers
2000: Oakland A's
2001: Seattle Mariners
2002: Oakland A's
2003: Oakland A's
2004: Anaheim Angels
2005: Los Angeles Angels of Anaheim
2006: Oakland A's
2007: Los Angeles Angels of Anaheim
* Strike-shortened season; no play-offs.

by the A's and Angels. Under general manager Billy Beane, Oakland has found a winning formula for keeping its payroll low while putting together a very competitive team. In the 2000s, A's teams have featured such excellent pitchers as Barry Zito, Mark Mulder, Tim Hudson, Dan Haren, and Huston Street. Top position players during this successful stretch included Jason Giambi, Miguel Tejada, and Eric Chavez. Only a couple of these players are still with the A's, as players' success usually leads them to become high-priced free agents. At that point, Beane deals them to a ball club with deeper pockets, often picking up some great young talented players in the trade. Beane's surprising success at doing business this way became the subject of a bestselling book called *Moneyball*.

Following their World Series championship in 2002, the Anaheim Angels continued their winning ways, at least during the regular season. In 2005, the team changed its name to the Los Angeles Angels of Anaheim and went on to win the division title in two of the next three years. Unfortunately, the Angels have not fared well in the playoffs. During their recent success, the team was led by 2004 American League MVP Vladimir Guerrero, All-Star left fielder Garret Anderson, pitching ace John Lackey, and super closer Frankie Rodriguez. With their recent winning tradition and big-market deep pockets, expect the Angels to be contenders for a long time to come.

# CHAPTER TWO
# THE PLAYERS

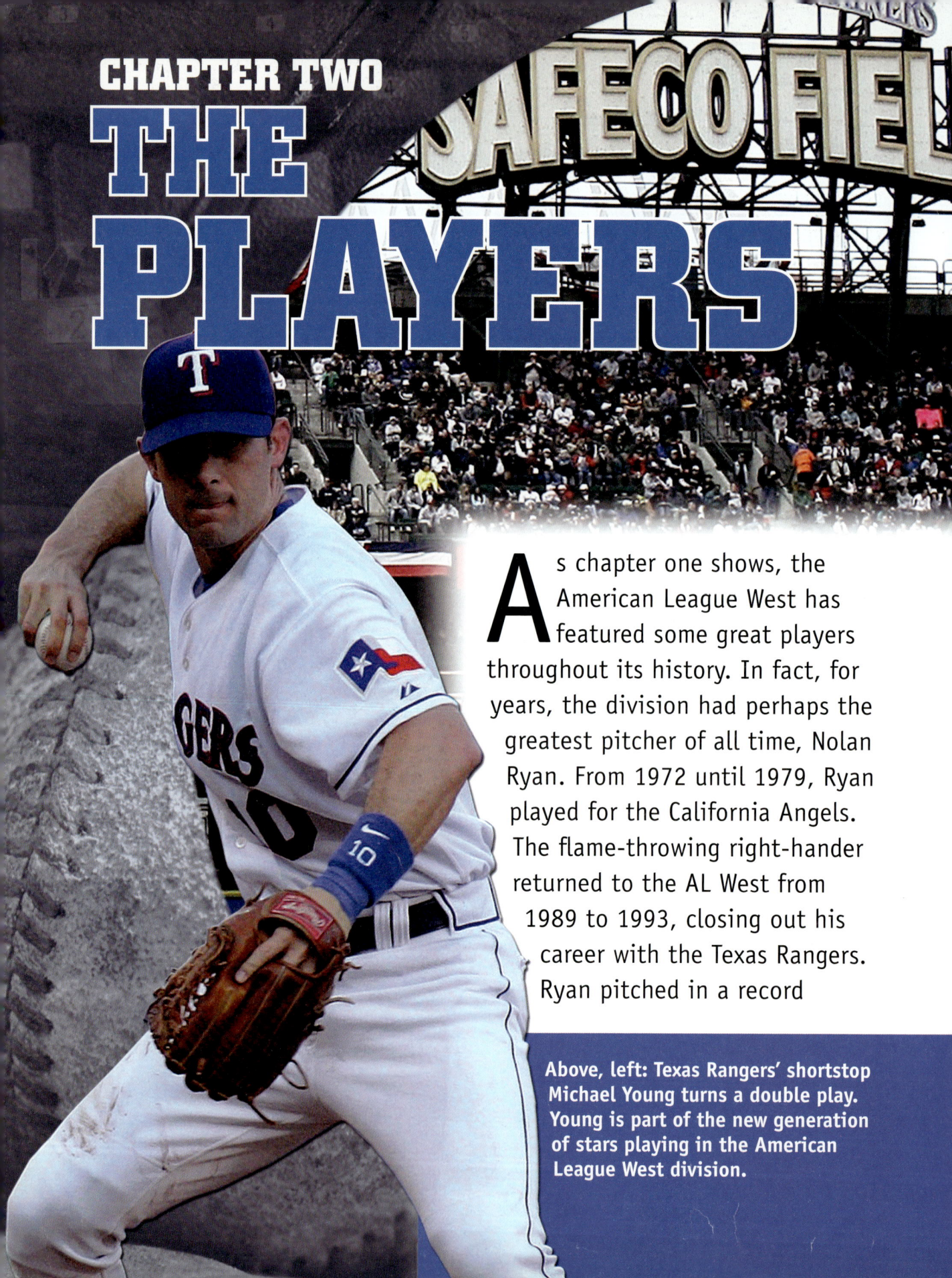

As chapter one shows, the American League West has featured some great players throughout its history. In fact, for years, the division had perhaps the greatest pitcher of all time, Nolan Ryan. From 1972 until 1979, Ryan played for the California Angels. The flame-throwing right-hander returned to the AL West from 1989 to 1993, closing out his career with the Texas Rangers. Ryan pitched in a record

Above, left: Texas Rangers' shortstop Michael Young turns a double play. Young is part of the new generation of stars playing in the American League West division.

27 seasons, winning 324 games, and setting the record for career strikeouts, with 5,714. He also threw an incredible seven no-hitters, three more than runner-up Sandy Koufax. Ryan was inducted into the Hall of Fame in 1999.

Since 1994, several players have stood out from the pack, bringing their best to every game and continuing the tradition of hard-nosed, exciting AL West baseball. This chapter profiles some of these players.

## Ken Griffey Jr. (Mariners)

In the 1987 amateur draft, the Seattle Mariners' first overall selection was a highly touted player named Ken Griffey Jr. Landing this great young star would mark a sea change in Mariners history. From his rookie season in 1989 through 1999, Griffey hammered baseballs all over the Seattle Superdome, piling up hits, home runs, and RBI at an impressive rate. In addition, he was one of the most exciting outfielders in the game. He won eleven consecutive Gold Glove Awards for outstanding defensive play.

In 1995, Ken Griffey Jr. and pitcher Randy Johnson led the Mariners to the AL West title. The team went on to beat the New York Yankees in the new American League Division Series. Two years later, Griffey won the American League MVP Award, batting .304, smashing 56 home runs and driving in 147 runs. Junior, as he is known, was traded to the Cincinnati Reds following the 1999 season.

## Ivan Rodriguez (Rangers)

In the late 1990s, Texas was the team to beat in the AL West. Led by the hitting of All-Stars Ivan Rodriguez and Juan González, the team

Ivan "Pudge" Rodriguez watches the flight of a ball during a game in 1999, the season in which he won the American League MVP Award. His Rangers finished at the top of the AL West division that year.

piled up a ton of runs. Unfortunately, the Rangers' pitching didn't quite live up to its offense, and the Rangers never advanced in the postseason.

For 12 seasons, the Rangers' catcher Ivan "Pudge" Rodriguez was the team's steady superstar. Many believe he is the best catcher ever. Between 1992 and 2001, Rodriguez won 10 consecutive Gold Glove Awards. In addition, he was selected to the All-Star team in each of those 10 years. Rodriguez threw out nearly 50 percent of the runners who attempted to steal against him. (An average catcher throws out about 25 percent!)

Impressively, Rodriguez's defensive skills were matched by his batting skills. Rodriguez holds the American League record for home runs by a catcher (35, in 1999) as well as the MLB record for most doubles in a season by a catcher (47, in 1996). His career batting average is over .300, which is very rare for a catcher. In 1999, Rodriguez was named American League MVP. He batted .332 that year, scored 116 runs, and belted 35 home runs with 113 RBI. For good measure, he also stole 25 bases, a record for catchers. After the 2002 season, Rodriguez became a free agent and signed with the Florida Marlins of the National League.

## Vladimir Guerrero (Angels)

In the 2000s, Montreal Expos outfielder Vladimir Guerrero was one of the hottest young stars in the game. Following the 2003 season, the Expos traded Guerrero to the Anaheim Angels. In his first year with the club, Guerrero put together one of the best hitting seasons in recent memory. He batted .337, hit 39 home runs, and drove in 126 runs.

The Angels' Vladimir Guerrero unleashes a mighty swing. Guerrero is one of the most consistent sluggers in the game, averaging more than 30 home runs and 100 RBI per season over his career.

He also led the league with 366 total bases and 124 runs scored. Guerrero's late-season hitting led the Angels to the West division title and sealed his selection as the 2004 American League MVP.

Since 2004, Guerrero has continued to live up to his reputation as a ferocious power hitter who can take any pitch and smack it into the stands. In addition, he is viewed as one of the game's true "five-tool" players, with exceptional skills at hitting for average, hitting for power, fielding, throwing, and running.

Guerrero is one of the few major league hitters who do not wear batting gloves. He says his hands got tough as a youngster, when he worked with cattle on his grandfather's ranch in his native Dominican Republic.

## Michael Young (Rangers)

Since his rookie season in 2001, shortstop Michael Young has impressed Rangers fans with both his hitting and slick fielding. A four-time All-Star, Young registered five consecutive 200-hit seasons between 2003 and 2007, and he shows no sign of slowing down. Young is regularly among the American League's top hitters, and he led the league with a .331 average in 2005.

## Eric Chavez (A's)

From 2001 to 2006, Oakland's Eric Chavez played his third base position better than any other player, winning six consecutive Gold Glove Awards. Chavez is always a threat at the plate as well. On a team historically known for its big hitters, Chavez ranks among the top ten on the Oakland career lists for home runs, RBI, and total bases. Injured late in the 2007 season, Chavez is expected to return to the A's lineup to add to his impressive career totals.

## Ichiro Suzuki (Mariners)

Playing for the Orix Blue Wave in the Japanese Pacific League, Ichiro Suzuki established himself as Japan's best all-around player. He won seven consecutive batting titles and seven consecutive Gold Glove Awards. In 2001, the Seattle Mariners signed Ichiro to a three-year contract, making him the first Japanese-born position player in the major leagues. Unbelievably, upon arriving in the United States, his game got even better.

The twenty-seven-year-old Ichiro made an immediate impact, winning the 2001 Rookie of the Year Award and earning the American League MVP Award. He led the league in batting, with a .350 average, and in stolen bases, with 56. He won a Gold Glove Award that year, and he has won a Gold Glove Award every season since. Ichiro's throwing arm in right field may be the strongest and most accurate of any player in either league.

In 2004, Ichiro put on one of the greatest hitting displays ever. He set the record for most hits in a season (262), including most singles (215), and finished with a major league–best average of .376. He had 80 multi-hit games, including 24 three-hit games, six four-hit games, and four five-hit games!

## Francisco Rodriguez (Angels)

Originally from Venezuela, Frankie Rodriguez became an overnight sensation in the 2002 postseason. At just 21 years old, he pitched

Seattle's Ichiro Suzuki bats in the 2004 All-Star Game at Minute Maid Park in Houston, Texas. In each of his first three years, Ichiro received more All-Star votes than any other player.

the Angels to postseason victories over the Yankees, Twins, and San Francisco Giants on the way to a World Series title. Rodriguez has lived up to his early brilliance. In 2005, he saved 45 games in 50 opportunities, and in 2006 he recorded 47 saves in 51 opportunities, with a 1.73 ERA. Those gaudy numbers earned him the 2006 American League Rolaids Relief Man of the Year Award. Rodriguez was voted onto the All-Star team for a second time in 2007.

## Young Guns of the Wild West

Teams in the American League West division have been producing great players for 40 years now. As the division enters its fifth decade of existence, a host of young stars promises to keep baseball exciting in the AL West.

### John Lackey (Angels)

In 2007, the Angels right-hander went 19-9, throwing 224 innings. He led American League starters in earned run average (3.01) and came in third in voting for the American League Cy Young Award, which honors the league's best pitcher.

### Félix Hernández (Mariners)

With a blazing fastball and great off-speed stuff to match, "King Felix" is one of the brightest young stars in baseball. In 2006, at the tender age of 20 years old, Hernandez led the Mariners' pitching staff with 12 victories and 176 strikeouts. In 2007, he had the lowest ERA among the Mariners' starters and again led the team in strikeouts. Seattle hopes he'll be the team's ace for many years to come.

Mariners' ace Félix Hernández delivers a pitch in a 2008 game against the Oakland A's. The young Venezuelan-born star regularly hits 100 MPH on the radar gun.

### J. J. Putz (Mariners)

J. J. Putz became Seattle's closer in 2006, recording an impressive 36 saves for the last-place Mariners. That year, he led American League relievers with 104 strikeouts, while walking only 13. In 2007, the big right-hander was selected to his first All-Star team and took home the Rolaids Relief Man of the Year Award. He notched 40 saves in 42 tries, had a 6-1 record, and recorded a miniscule 1.38 ERA.

### Huston Street (A's)

Oakland's young right-hander has earned a reputation as one of the best closers in baseball. In 2005, Street earned American League Rookie of the Year honors. He pitched his way to a 5-1 record and saved 23 games in 27 opportunities. His ERA of 1.72 was the best in the AL West.

Seattle's J. J. Putz delivers to the plate in 2008. Between the end of 2006 and the beginning of 2007, Putz recorded 31 consecutive saves, a Mariners record.

## American League West Award Winners
### (since realignment in 1994)

### American League MVP Award
1996 Juan González (Rangers)
1997 Ken Griffey Jr. (Mariners)
1998 Juan González (Rangers)
1999 Ivan Rodriguez (Rangers)
2000 Jason Giambi (A's)
2001 Ichiro Suzuki (Mariners)
2002 Miguel Tejada (A's)
2003 Alex Rodriguez (Rangers)
2004 Vladimir Guerrero (Angels)

### American League Rookie of the Year Award
1998 Ben Grieve (A's)
2000 Kazuhiro Sasaki (Mariners)
2001 Ichiro Suzuki (Mariners)
2004 Bobby Crosby (A's)
2005 Huston Street (A's)

### American League Cy Young Award
1995 Randy Johnson (Mariners)
2002 Barry Zito (A's)
2005 Bartolo Colon (Angels)

### Rolaids Relief Man of the Year Award
2002 Billy Koch (A's)
2003 Keith Foulke (A's)
2006 Francisco Rodriguez (Angels)
2007 J. J. Putz (Mariners)

### World Series MVP Award
2002 Troy Glaus (Angels)

## CHAPTER THREE
# MEMORABLE GAMES

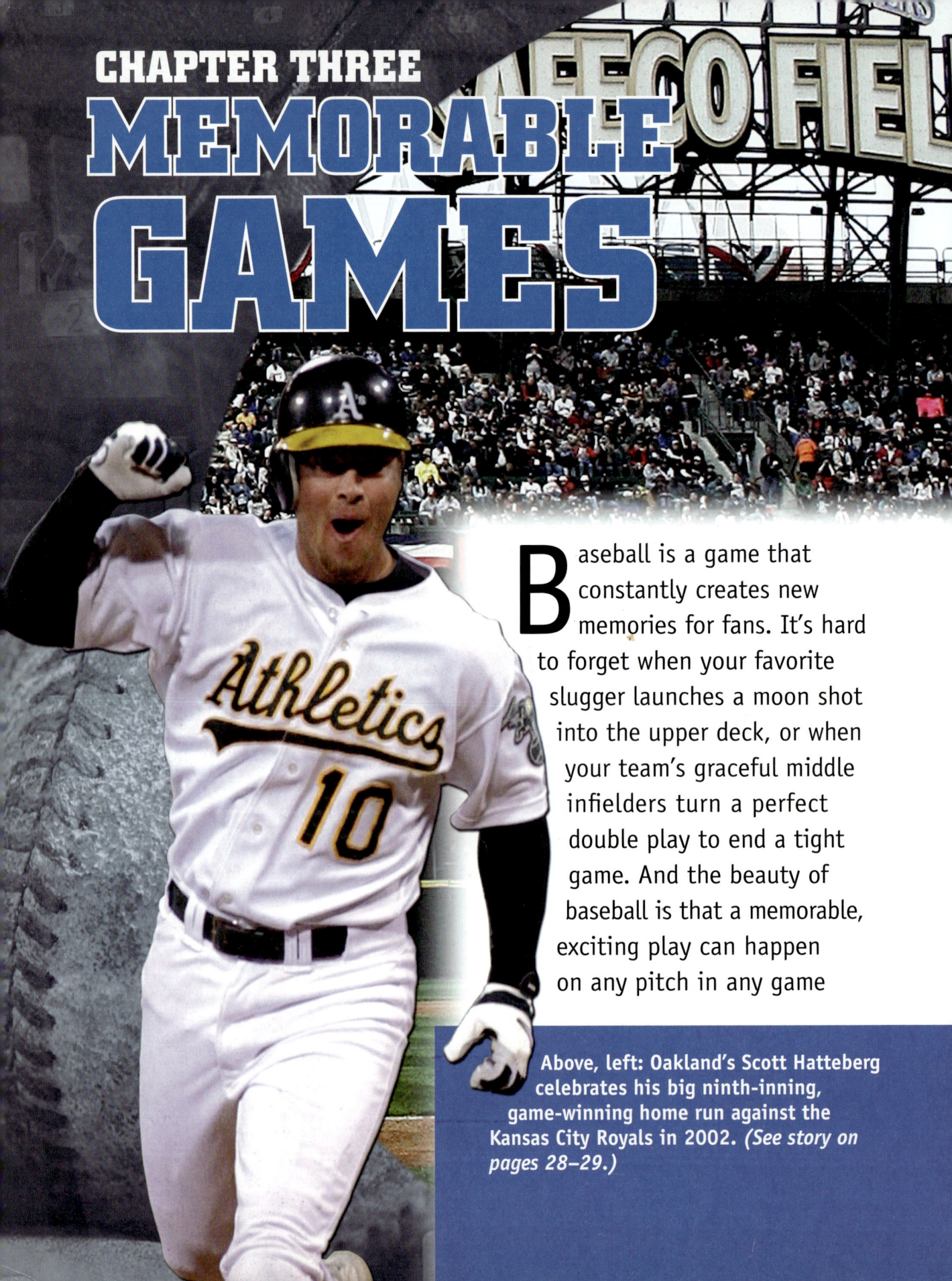

Baseball is a game that constantly creates new memories for fans. It's hard to forget when your favorite slugger launches a moon shot into the upper deck, or when your team's graceful middle infielders turn a perfect double play to end a tight game. And the beauty of baseball is that a memorable, exciting play can happen on any pitch in any game

*Above, left:* Oakland's Scott Hatteberg celebrates his big ninth-inning, game-winning home run against the Kansas City Royals in 2002. *(See story on pages 28–29.)*

MEMORABLE GAMES

throughout the long season. The games profiled in this chapter give you just a taste of some of the recent memorable moments involving teams from the AL West division.

## Mariners' Miracle Year

Early in August 1995, the Los Angeles Angels led the AL West division by 11 games and seemed a shoo-in for the post-season. However, the team suffered two nine-game losing streaks in the following weeks and gave up first place. As the Angels fell apart, the Seattle Mariners surged to the top of the division, led by the hitting of Edgar Martinez and Ken Griffey Jr. The Mariners also had the hottest pitcher in baseball, Randy "Big Unit" Johnson. The lanky left-hander would win the American League Cy Young Award that year with an 18-2 record, a 2.48 ERA, and 294 strikeouts.

The Angels and Rangers ended up with identical

The Mariners converge on the pitching mound to mob winning pitcher Randy Johnson, as the team celebrates its 1995 American League West division championship.

BASEBALL IN THE AMERICAN LEAGUE WEST DIVISION

78-66 records. (The season was shortened by the 1994 players' strike, which carried on into the beginning of 1995.) For the one-game play-off for the division title, Johnson threw a complete game, and his team drubbed the hapless Angels by a 9–1 score. With the win, the Mariners moved on to the first ever postseason series in the team's nineteen-year history.

## "Everybody Scores!"

The 1995 one-game play-off between the Mariners and Angels featured an unusual play and one of the more memorable radio calls in recent history. In the seventh inning, with Seattle clinging to a slim 1–0 lead, the Mariners' light-hitting backup infielder Luis Sojo came to the plate with two outs and the bases loaded. Many Seattle fans will forever remember the frenzied call by radio play-by-play announcer Rick Rizzs: "Here's the pitch, swing, and it's a ground ball up the first base line and it gets on by Snow! Down the right field line into the bullpen! Here comes Blowers! Here comes Tino! Here comes Joey! The throw to the plate, cut off! The relay behind Langston gets on by Allanson! Cora scores! Here comes Sojo, he scores! Everybody scores!"

## A's Win Twenty in a Row

In late summer of 2002, no team in baseball was hotter than the Oakland A's. Led by star pitchers Barry Zito and Tim Hudson and the hot bat of All-Star shortstop Miguel Tejada, the A's put together an amazing winning streak. The team entered its September 4 game with the Kansas City Royals not having lost since August 12. With their 19 straight wins, the A's sat tied for the longest winning streak in AL history. A win against the Royals would give the A's a new record in the modern (post-1900) era.

To the delight of the hometown crowd, the A's jumped out to a huge 11-0 lead by the third inning. However, the Royals scored five runs in the fourth and five more in the eighth and then tied the score with two runs in the top of the ninth! On the brink of a disappointing collapse, A's pinch hitter Scott Hatteberg came to bat in the bottom of the ninth inning and clocked a solo homer into the right-field stands. The scene of Hatteberg getting mobbed as he reached home plate is one that A's fans will not soon forget. The record-setting 12–11 win was the last in the team's magical streak, as the Minnesota Twins shut out the A's 6–0 in their next game.

## Rangers' Modern-Day Record for Runs Scored

On August 22, 2007, the Texas Rangers took on the Baltimore Orioles in the first game of a doubleheader. When the dust settled, the final tally looked more like a football blowout than a baseball score: 30–3. The Rangers put up five runs in the fourth inning, nine runs in the sixth, 10 in the eighth, and six more in the ninth. The 30 runs were the most in the modern era of the major leagues and set a new American League record.

At the time, the Rangers did not have what would be considered a high-powered offense. In fact, the team had scored a total of only 28 runs in its previous nine games. On this afternoon, however, Rangers bats were on fire. They got two homers and seven RBI each from Jarrod Saltalamacchia and Ramón Vázquez, batting in the bottom two spots in the lineup. In addition, the Rangers' Travis Metcalf and Marlon Byrd each hit grand slams. Rangers starting pitcher Kason Gabbard earned the easy win. Talk about run support!

# CHAPTER FOUR
# BALLPARKS AND TRADITIONS

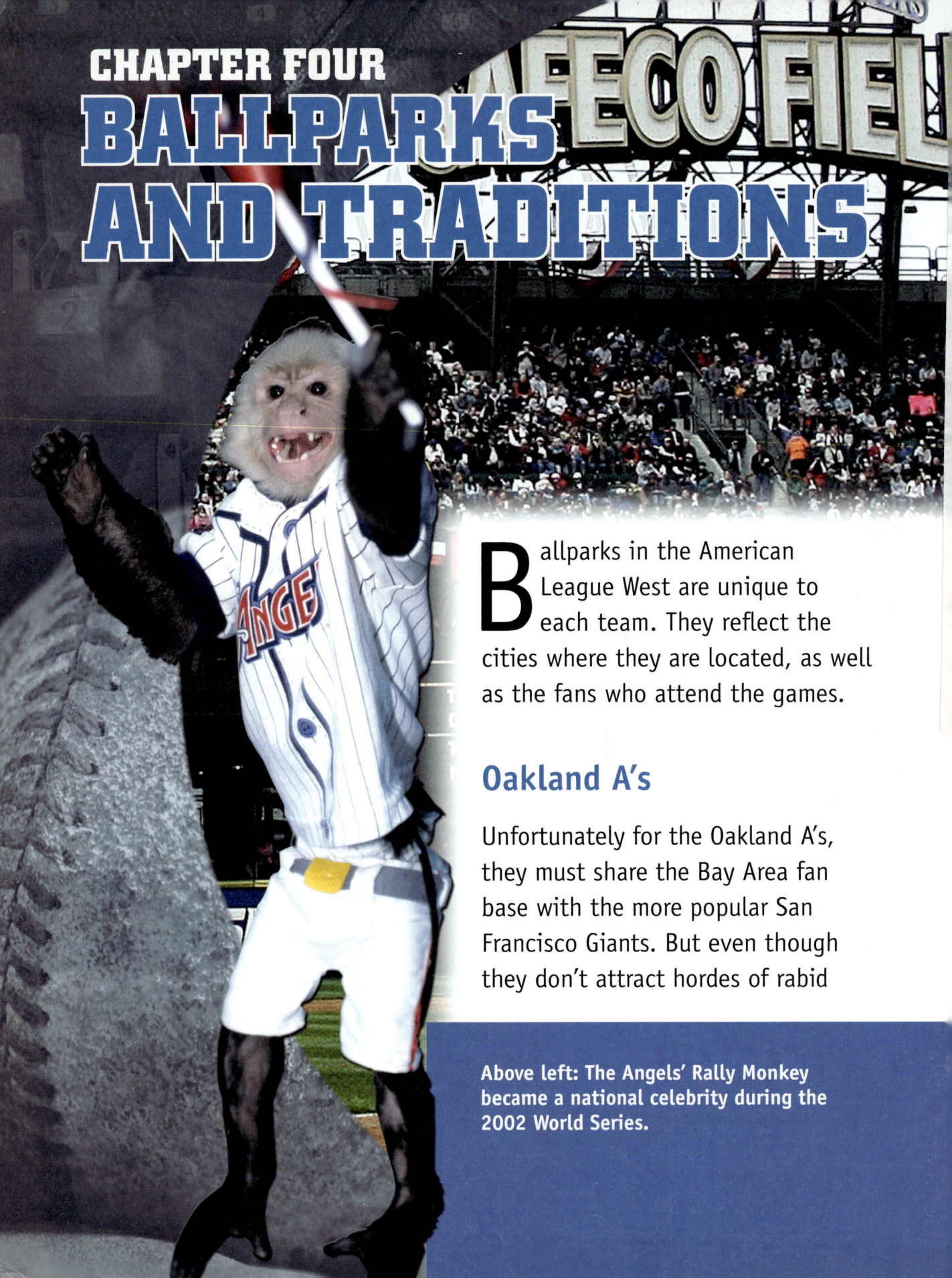

Ballparks in the American League West are unique to each team. They reflect the cities where they are located, as well as the fans who attend the games.

## Oakland A's

Unfortunately for the Oakland A's, they must share the Bay Area fan base with the more popular San Francisco Giants. But even though they don't attract hordes of rabid

**Above left:** The Angels' Rally Monkey became a national celebrity during the 2002 World Series.

BALLPARKS AND TRADITIONS

Three of the four teams in the American League West division are located in cities along the West Coast. Arlington, on the other hand, is located in hot, humid northeast Texas.

fans like the Giants, the A's have consistently put a winner on the field throughout their history.

### McAfee Coliseum (formerly Oakland-Alameda County Coliseum)
**Location:** Oakland, California
**Opened for baseball in:** 1968
**Surface:** Natural grass
**Seating capacity:** 34,077 (smallest capacity in the major leagues)

Spectacular opening-day ceremonies are a tradition in baseball. Here, players and coaches line up for the national anthem prior to the 2007 opening-night game at Oakland's McAfee Coliseum.

Oakland built Alameda County Coliseum in 1966 in order to lure Charlie Finley's Athletics team away from Kansas City. Designed for both football and baseball, the Coliseum held 48,219 spectators. In spite of its huge seating capacity, the Coliseum never drew huge numbers of baseball fans. In 2006, the third-level bleachers were closed in an attempt to make the field better for baseball. This reduced the seating capacity to 34,077, the smallest seating capacity in the major leagues.

McAfee Coliseum is considered a pitcher's park. Expansive foul territory allows defensive players to catch balls that would land well into the stands at many other parks. The park was the setting for a perfect game thrown by Oakland's Catfish Hunter against the Minnesota Twins in 1968, as well as Rickey Henderson's record-breaking 939th stolen base in 1991. A new stadium for the Oakland A's, Cisco Park, is planned for the opening of the 2011 season.

## Texas Rangers

The Rangers baseball team was named in honor of the Texas Rangers, a law enforcement group whose history dates back to the gun-slinging "Wild West" days of the 1820s. Many ballparks play the traditional "Take Me Out to the Ballgame" song during the seventh-inning stretch. Fans at Rangers Ballpark, however, also enjoy dancing to the country-western song "Cotton-Eyed Joe."

### Rangers Ballpark
**Location:** Arlington, Texas
**Opened in:** 1994

**Surface:** Natural grass
**Seating capacity:** 49,115

The Rangers' original ballpark, Turnpike Stadium, was a minor-league park built in 1965. In 1970, the stadium was renamed Arlington Stadium and upgraded to attract the failing Washington Senators franchise. From 1972 to 1993, the Rangers played at Arlington Stadium. Construction on a new park began in 1992, spearheaded by part-owner and future U.S. president George W. Bush. It opened for baseball in 1994.

The granite and brick exterior of the beautiful new Ballpark at Arlington recalls the classic old stadiums from the early days of baseball.

BALLPARKS AND TRADITIONS

The renovated Rangers Ballpark is one of the more hitter-friendly parks in baseball. Arlington's high temperatures and low humidity allow balls to travel well, and the park has relatively short fences. The facility was designed to remind fans of old-time ballparks. Its features include a traditional exterior, an asymmetrical playing field,

## Retro Classics

Throughout the 1960s and 1970s, many new sports stadiums were built to accommodate both football and baseball games. This meant the structures were often huge, doughnut-shaped monstrosities built off of a freeway for easy access. In these "space age" stadiums, four or even five tiers of spectator seating might rise above an artificial playing surface with perfectly symmetrical (even on all sides) field dimensions. As a result, baseball games in these structures were much less fun to watch. Gone were the intimacy and fan involvement that had made baseball the "great American pastime" in the first place. All that began to change in 1992, when the Baltimore Orioles opened their new field.

The construction of the Orioles' Camden Yards began a movement toward new, baseball-only parks that tried to capture a retro-classic feeling. Unlike the massive, round football stadiums, these new fields were being built right into the structure of their host cities. Construction plans called for open breaks beyond the walls in the outfield, allowing spectators to take in local landmarks and unique features of nearby buildings. Seating in the new parks was arranged specifically for good baseball sightlines and to get fans closer to the action. In addition, field dimensions were purposely made asymmetrical, or uneven, with odd corners and wall angles, making hits to the outfield much more unpredictable and harder to field. These features reminded fans of the great old baseball-only ballparks like Fenway Park in Boston and Wrigley Field in Chicago.

Three of the four ballparks in the American League West—Rangers Ballpark, Angel Stadium, and Safeco Field—have elements of the retro-classic ballparks.

and a friendly home-run porch in right field. The ballpark complex also houses the Legends of the Game Baseball Museum.

## Seattle Mariners

From their first season in 1977 through 1990, the Mariners failed to achieve a winning record. Their fortunes began to change in the 1990s, however. After rebuilding a team around Ken Griffey Jr. and Randy Johnson, the Mariners put together a decade of fun and entertaining baseball. Unfortunately, the Mariners' home ballpark, the Kingdome, was neither a fun nor entertaining place to watch a baseball game. It was built with football games in mind. Beautiful Safeco Field replaced the Kingdome as the Mariners' home field in 1999.

### Safeco Field

**Location:** Seattle, Washington
**Opened in:** 1999
**Surface:** Natural grass
**Seating capacity:** 47,116

Safeco is sometimes called the "House that Griffey Built." This is because Ken Griffey Jr. was the face of the Mariners organization as the city of Seattle raised funds for construction. (The state-of-the-art park cost more than $500 million.)

One of the most interesting features of Safeco Field is its roof, which was designed specially for the rainy weather that is typical in Seattle in the summer. The roof covers the field like an umbrella but does not enclose it. The roof can be retracted when the weather is nice, or it can be extended to cover the field when it rains.

This view of lush Safeco Field in Seattle shows the stadium's massive retractable roof *(upper right)*. The dark wall in center field provides batters with a good background to see the pitched ball.

## American League West Team History
### (since realignment in 1994)

| | YEAR ENTERED THE AL WEST | AL WEST CHAMPIONSHIPS | AL WEST PENNANTS | WORLD SERIES CHAMPIONSHIPS |
|---|---|---|---|---|
| Los Angeles Angels of Anaheim | 1969 | 3 | 1 | 1 |
| Oakland Athletics | 1969 | 4 | 0 | 0 |
| Seattle Mariners | 1977 | 3 | 0 | 0 |
| Texas Rangers | 1972 | 4* | 0 | 0 |

* Includes 1994; Texas was in first place in the division when the players' strike ended the season.

## Los Angeles Angels of Anaheim

Originally, the Angels were called the Los Angeles Angels and played at Wrigley Field in Los Angeles (not to be confused with the more famous Wrigley Field in Chicago). For the 1965 season, the Angels changed their name to the California Angels, to broaden their appeal throughout the entire state. However, the Disney Corporation bought controlling interest in the team in 1997. Its owners insisted that the team name include the name "Anaheim," the location of the amusement park Disneyland. Say hello to the Anaheim Angels. Later, when a new Angels owner wanted his team to appeal to the largest nearby market, he insisted that the team name include "Los Angeles." Thus was born the Los Angeles Angels of Anaheim. No wonder they just want to be called the "Angels"!

## Angel Stadium of Anaheim

**Location:** Anaheim, California
**Opened in:** 1966
**Surface:** Natural grass
**Seating capacity:** 40,050

Anaheim Stadium, which opened in 1966, quickly became known as "the Big A," for the huge, distinctive A-shaped scoreboard that rose above left field. Beginning in 1980, the Angels shared their stadium with the Los Angeles Rams of the National Football League. This arrangement required the stadium to be enclosed to add thousands of seats for football spectators. However, the Rams moved to St. Louis after the 1994 season, and major renovations were begun in 1996 to turn the Big A back into a baseball-only field. The newly renovated park, renamed Angel Stadium of Anaheim, was ready in time for the opening of the 1998 season.

Among the unique features of the park is a rock outcropping and running water beyond the fence in left field. As of 2007, the upgraded ballpark has hosted four American League Division Series (2002, 2004, 2005, and 2007) and two American League Championship Series (2002 and 2005). Notably, Angel Stadium hosted the 2002 World Series, which the Angels won, with the help of the now-famous Rally Monkey.

# GLOSSARY

**asymmetrical**  Not evenly proportioned.
**cleats**  Shoes with spikes used for baseball.
**debut**  First appearance.
**despise**  To hate.
**executive**  Person who has administrative or managerial control.
**expansive**  Sizeable; extensive.
**fiasco**  Sudden and violent collapse.
**free agent**  Player who is not under contract and can sign with whichever team offers the most money.
**gaudy**  Glaring or eye-catching; also, exceptional.
**gimmick**  Ingenious and usually new scheme or ploy.
**hapless**  Prone to failure.
**horde**  Large group of people.
**insurmountable**  Unable to be beaten or topped.
**miniscule**  Tiny; very small.
**perennial**  Occurring every year.
**retract**  To pull back.
**rivalry**  Intense competition between two teams.
**sea change**  Great transformation.
**shoo-in**  One that is a certain and easy winner.
**tout**  To praise, usually extravagantly and publicly.
**watershed**  Turning point.

# FOR MORE INFORMATION

Major League Baseball
The Office of the Commissioner of Baseball
245 Park Avenue, 31st Floor
New York, NY 10167
(212) 931-7800
Web site: http://www.mlb.com
The commissioner's office oversees all aspects of Major League Baseball.

National Baseball Hall of Fame and Museum
25 Main Street
Cooperstown, NY 13326
(888) HALL-OF-FAME (425-5633)
Web site: http://www.baseballhalloffame.org
The National Baseball Hall of Fame and Museum celebrates and preserves the history of baseball.

Negro Leagues Baseball Museum
1616 East 18th Street
Kansas City, MO 64108
(816) 221-1920
Web site: http://www.nlbm.com
The Negro Leagues Baseball Museum honors great African American baseball players who were once excluded from Major League Baseball.

(Note: Links to official team Web sites are available at the Rosenlinks URL, listed below.)

## Web Sites

Due to the changing nature of Internet links, Rosen Publishing has developed an online list of Web sites related to the subject of this book. This site is updated regularly. Please use this link to access the list:

http://www.rosenlinks.com/imlb/amlw

# FOR FURTHER READING

Altergott, Hannah. *Great Teams in Baseball History*. Milwaukee, WI: Raintree Publishing, 2006.

Christopher, Matt. *World Series: Legendary Sports Events*. New York, NY: Little, Brown & Company, 2007.

Fischer, David. *Baseball Top 10*. New York, NY: DK Publishing, Inc., 2004.

Formosa, Dan, and Paul Hamburger. *Baseball Field Guide: An In-Depth Illustrated Guide to the Complete Rules of Baseball*. New York, NY: Thunder's Mouth Press, 2006.

Light, Jonathan Fraser. *The Cultural Encyclopedia of Baseball*. Jefferson, NC: McFarland & Company, 2005.

Lipsyte, Robert. *Heroes of Baseball: The Men Who Made It America's Favorite Game*. New York, NY: Atheneum Books for Young Readers, 2006.

Mulroy, Kevin. *Baseball as America: Seeing Ourselves Through Our National Game*. Washington, D.C.: National Geographic Society, 2005.

Thiel, Art. *Out of Left Field: How the Mariners Made Baseball Fly in Seattle*. Seattle, WA: Sasquatch Books, 2003.

Thorn, John, ed., et al. *Total Baseball, Completely Revised and Updated: The Ultimate Baseball Encyclopedia*. Wilmington, DE: SportClassic Books, 2004.

Vecsey, George. *Baseball: A History of America's Favorite Game*. New York, NY: Random House Publishing Group, 2006.

# BIBLIOGRAPHY

Baseball Almanac. "World Series Most Valuable Player Award." 2008. Retrieved April 9, 2008 (http://www.baseball-almanac.com/awards/aw_mvpw.shtml).

BaseballLibrary.com. "League American." 2006. Retrieved April 10, 2008 (http://www.baseballlibrary.com/ballplayers/player.php?name=American_League).

BaseballReference.com. Multiple pages. Retrieved April 9–14, 2008 (http://www.baseball-reference.com).

Bauman, Mike. "Patience Will Pay Off for Rangers." MLB.com, March 17, 2008. Retrieved April 15, 2008 (http://texas.rangers.mlb.com/news/article_perspectives.jsp?ymd=20080317&content_id=2436171&vkey=perspectives&fext=.jsp).

Bradley, Jeff. "East2West." *ESPN The Magazine,* May 31, 2001.

Gillette, Gary, and Pete Palmer, eds. *The ESPN Baseball Encyclopedia*. Fifth ed. New York, NY: Sterling Publishing Co., 2008.

Grant, Evan. "Record Rout: Rangers Win, 30–3." DallasNews.com, August 23, 2007. Retrieved April 15, 2008 (http://www.dallasnews.com/sharedcontent/dws/dn/latestnews/stories/082307dnsporanglede.2a049d8.html).

JockBio.com. "Vladimir Guerrero." 2005. Retrieved April 11, 2008 (http://www.jockbio.com/Bios/Vlad/Vlad_bio.html).

# BIBLIOGRAPHY

Koppett, Leonard. *Koppett's Concise History of Major League Baseball*. New York, NY: Carroll & Graf Publishers, 2004.

Light, Jonathan Fraser. *The Cultural Encyclopedia of Baseball*. Jefferson, NC: McFarland & Company, 2005.

MLB.com. "Angel Stadium of Anaheim." 2008. Retrieved April 14, 2008 (http://losangeles.angels.mlb.com/ana/ballpark/index.jsp).

MLB.com. "McAfee Coliseum." 2008. Retrieved April 14, 2008 (http://oakland.athletics.mlb.com/oak/ballpark/index.jsp).

MLB.com. "Rangers Ballpark in Arlington: Home of the Rangers." 2008. Retrieved April 14, 2008 (http://rangers.mlb.com/tex/ballpark/index.jsp).

MLB.com. "Safeco Field." 2008. Retrieved April 14, 2008 (http://seattle.mariners.mlb.com/sea/ballpark/index.jsp).

MLB-Players.com. "Los Angeles Angels History." Retrieved April 14, 2008 (http://www.mlb-players.com/angels/angelshistory.php).

MLB-Players.com. "Oakland Athletics History." Retrieved April 14, 2008 (http://www.mlb-players.com/athletics/athleticshistory.php).

MLB-Players.com. "Seattle Mariners History." Retrieved April 14, 2008 (http://www.mlb-players.com/mariners/marinershistory.php).

MLB-Players.com. "Texas Rangers History." Retrieved April 14, 2008 (http://www.mlb-players.com/rangers/rangershistory.php).

Rolaids Relief Man Award Site. "Past Winners." 2007. Retrieved April 1, 2008 (http://www.rolaidsreliefman.com/pastwinners.aspx).

Wise, Mike. "A's Run Out of Rallies as Streak Ends at 20." *New York Times*, September 7, 2002.

# INDEX

## A
All-Stars, 13, 15, 17, 19, 22, 24, 28
amateur draft, 15
American League West
    ballparks, 11, 15, 30, 33–36, 38–39
    history, 6, 7–13
    memorable games, 26–29
    players, 14–15, 17, 19–20, 22, 24–25
    traditions, 4–5, 30, 33–36, 38–39
Anaheim Angels, 4–6, 13, 17, 19, 22, 27–28, 38–39

## C
California Angels, 10, 12–13, 14
Cy Young Awards, 22, 25, 27

## D
designated hitter rule, 9
Disney Corporation, 38

## G
Gold Glove Awards, 15, 17, 19, 20

## K
Kansas City Royals, 6, 8, 10, 11, 28–29

## L
League Championship Series (LCS), 8, 11, 39

## M
Major League Players' Union, 12
Minnesota Twins, 6, 8, 10, 11, 29
Mustache Gang, 9

## O
Oakland A's, 6, 8, 9, 10, 12–13, 19, 24, 28–29, 30–31, 33

## P
players' strike (1994), 11–12, 28

## R
Rally Monkey, 4–5, 39
Rolaids Relief Man of the Year Awards, 22, 24, 25
Rookie of the Year Awards, 20, 24, 25

## S
San Francisco Giants, 4–6, 11
Seattle Mariners, 6, 10, 12, 15, 20, 22, 24, 27–28, 36

## T
"Take Me Out to the Ballgame," 33
Texas Rangers, 6, 12, 14, 15, 17, 19, 27–28, 29, 33–36

## W
wild card teams, 6, 11, 12
World Series, 4, 6, 7, 10, 11, 12, 13, 22, 25

## About the Author

Ed Eck is a writer and television producer for the world's biggest cable sports network. For his work, he has interviewed dozens of baseball players, managers, and team executives. Eck has also covered hundreds of Major League Baseball games, including the National League and American League Championships Series and the World Series. He grew up outside of New York City and currently resides with his family in Connecticut.

## Photo Credits

Cover (background), pp. 7, 14, 18, 24 26, 30 Otto Greule Jr./Getty Images; cover (right) Otto Greule Jr./Getty Images; cover (insets, top to bottom), p. 1 (insets) Jonathan Daniel/Getty Images, Otto Greule Jr./Getty Images, (2) Ronald Martinez/Getty Images; pp. 4–5 © Rachel Van Pelt; p. 5 Lisa Blumenfeld/Getty Images; p. 7 Diamond Images/Getty Images; pp. 9, 26 © AP Images; p. 11 Ron Vesely/MLB/Getty Images; p. 14 Ronald Martinez/Getty Images; p. 16 David Maxwell/AFP/Getty Images; pp. 21, 23 Jed Jacobsohn/Getty Images; p. 27 Therese Frare/AFP/Getty Images; p. 30 John Cordes/MLB Photots/Getty Images; p. 32 Justin Sullivan/Getty Images; p. 34 Ronald Martinez/Getty Images; p. 37 Jerry Driendl/Getty Images.

Designer: Sam Zavieh; Editor: Christopher Roberts
Photo Researcher: Amy Feinberg